Beautiful

AMBROTYPES

Beautiful
AMBROTYPES
Early Photographs

Introduction by Paul Cox
Edited by Heather Forbes

TRAVELLING LIGHT

19th Century Photography Series: Volume 1
Beautiful Ambrotypes
First published in 1989 by Travelling Light
Old Town Hall, Lavender Hill, GB-London SW11 5TG

© 1989 Travelling Light
Introduction © Paul Cox
Text based on a chapter by B.E.C. Haworth-Loomes first published in
Victorian Photography: A Collectors Guide, Ward Lock, London 1974.
Design by Edwina Fitzpatrick
Printed in Great Britain by The Roundwood Press Ltd., Warwick
Distributed in Great Britain by Central Books, 14 the Leathermarket, London SE1 3ER

CIP DATA
Beautiful ambrotypes: early photographs. — (19th century photographs).
   1. Photographs, 1800–1900
   I. Forbes, Heather, *1948–*   II. Series 770.9'034

ISBN 0-906333-25-3

Front cover Ambrotypes: Portrait of young Welsh girl taken in Blaina, Gwent.
                    Portrait of mother and daughter.
Back cover Ambrotype: Sir Charles Tilston Bright and family.

CONTENTS

INTRODUCTION

by Paul Cox

Well before the birth of motor-drives and automatic cameras Bernard Shaw said 'Photographers are like codfish that lay a million eggs in order to hatch one.' Nowadays photographers are a little like machine-gun operators 'you can't miss as long as you keep shooting.' Bernard Shaw would have been horrified! The child in us must never die. Our richest moments are those moments when we observe the world like a child; liberated from time, place and rationality. Unfortunately in modern times our children are conditioned to consume and consequently lose their ability 'to see'. This book is called *Beautiful Ambrotypes* and indeed these images are beautiful. They are beautiful because they have integrity, a completeness that projects itself well beyond the last century.

When one develops a photographic image the past becomes visible and merges with the present. It's a mystery forever fresh and new. Small things often haunt us; the smile of a child, a patch of light on the wall, a face in the crowd. Birth and death are separated by a leaf falling in autumn, a train hurrying through the night, a smile, a tear, the pain of too much tenderness. These ambrotypes project life as it really is and take on great richness the longer one looks at them. Maybe they can help us to recapture a little of the mystique of photography and the mystique of life. Our exterior world moves forward at an alarming speed but the heart and the imagination cannot follow them when the accepted formula is fast and pointless. *Beautiful Ambrotypes* help us to slow down a little so we can still love with our senses and our hearts.

Frederick Scott Archer

THE AMBROTYPE:
Invention and
Environment

In March of 1851, Frederick Scott Archer described a process that was to remain the principal method of photography for the next quarter of a century, superseding both the daguerrotype and calotype within a few years.

For an efficient employment of the negative-positive system, the support for the light sensitive chemicals had to be as transparent as possible; and glass was the obvious material. Niépce had used glass for his first successful heliographic copy of a drawing in 1822 and Herschel had taken a photograph on glass in 1839, but had found the process difficult and unsatisfactory. On the paper negatives, the chemicals had been absorbed into the fibres, and the problem with glass was to find a substance capable of holding the sensitive salts without impairing the transparency of the glass.

In 1847, Abel Niépce de Saint-Victor, a cousin of Nicéphore Niépce, had introduced a process in which the glass plate was coated with albumen and potassium iodide, and allowed to dry before before being sensitized with silver nitrate. Excellent results were obtained with landscapes and art reproductions, but the exposure times of five to fifteen minutes made portraiture almost impossible. This was a serious commercial failing, for portrait photography represented a major part of the professional photographer's work.

Archer had found photography a useful aid to accuracy in his work as a sculptor, having been instructed in the calotype process by his doctor, Hugh W. Diamond, in 1847. Within a short time, Archer had begun experiments to improve the quality of photographic paper and this work led him, in 1849, to the use of a recently discovered substance. In 1847, it had been shown that guncotton was soluble in ether and produced a sticky solution that was given the name 'collodion', from the Greek word for glue. Early suggestions for its use were in the field of surgery where it was thought that its transparency when dried and its strength of adhesion, coupled with the fact that it was impermeable to water, would make it an ideal dressing for wounds.

After various experiments, Archer decided to dispense with paper and use a film of collodion as a base for the light sensitive chemicals. In 1851, he published the details of his 'wet collodion process' in the March issue of *The Chemist*. A solution of collodion and potassium iodide was poured onto a clean glass plate and allowed to flow evenly over the surface. When sufficient of the ether had evaporated to leave a tacky residue, the plate was immersed in a bath of silver nitrate. Then, whilst wet, the plate was placed in the camera for exposure and the still moist negative developed with pyrogallic acid and fixed with hyposulphite of soda. Archer's original idea had been to peel the collodion film from the plate and store it around a glass rod for fixing later, but it was found that the collodion lacked the strength for this to be practical and photographers used fresh plates for each exposure.

For the travelling photographer, the equipment required was considerable. Each stage in the preparation of the plate, as well as the exposing and developing of the negative, had to be completed before the plate dried and became insensitive to light. This meant that a dark room had to be available, and portable tents complete with chemicals, storage space for water, dishes and glass plates were soon being offered for sale. Despite the handicap of bulky and heavy apparatus, photographers quickly adopted the new process that was capable of producing negatives of high quality after exposures of only a few seconds.

For the first time in England, a method of photography completely free of patent restrictions was available, for Archer had given his process to the world. For all his inventiveness and generosity, Archer received little recognition. His experiments had occupied much of his time at the expense of his profession, and for many years he had been in poor health. Some attempts were made to obtain a pension for him but these efforts met with no success, and he died in poverty aged forty-four in 1857.

Although amateurs had employed the daguerreotype and calotype processes, the cost and difficulties involved had deterred many from indulging in the art as a hobby. With the introduction of Archer's invention, photography entered into a period of increasing popularity. In 1851, there had

been about a dozen studios in London and by 1866 this number had increased to 284. Photographic societies were formed throughout the world and, although many were disbanded after a few years, some still survive. Edinburgh, London, Manchester and Paris are cities that possess societies formed during this period. Books, pamphlets and manuals offering instruction and advice in all branches of photography were published, and chemists' shops began their long association with photography by stocking the chemicals required by the amateur.

One of the leading photographic dealers, Horne & Thornthwaite, advertised over forty different cameras in their catalogue for 1857, ranging in price from 9s. to £31. 9s.

Photography as a hobby was mainly a middle-class luxury. Wages in Victorian times were low. A skilled farm worker would have received about 10s. 6d. a week, and, even in the cities, pay for highly regarded jobs on the railways, or in the police force as a constable, would only have been about £1 a week. On such wages, families could live adequately by the standards of the day, but relatively expensive hobbies such as photography were generally out of the question. However, with large numbers of studios opening all over the country and with even small villages being served by travelling photographers, the poorer section of the population could afford to have their photographs taken by a professional.

One of the popular processes used for portraiture was the *ambrotype* also known as the *wet-collodion positive* and *collodion positive on glass*, developed by Scott Archer and Peter W. Fry in 1851, although not in wide commercial use until 1855. Using nitric acid or bichloride of mercury, a collodion negative was bleached and placed over a dark backing or painted to give a positive effect. The portrait appeared laterally reversed as was common with earlier daguerreotype portraits. Similarly, the sizes and method of presentation were often identical to those used for the daguerrotype process. Although the wet-collodion process gave excellent results, it was messy, smelly and cumbersome. Photographers could be recognised by their blackened fingers caused by the use of silver nitrate and it was popularly described as the *black art*.

With a large number of studios competing for business, prices and quality varied considerably. Some photographers charged as little as 1s., and this may have included a cup of coffee for the sitter while the photograph was being developed and fixed. Among the better photographers, prices were from 2s. 6d. to 5s. depending on the size of the photograph. Frames or cases were extra and the prices for these were influenced by the extent of local competition. For the best-quality, decorated, Morocco leather cases with embossed silk-plush linings, complete with brass mounts and glass, in a popular size of $3\frac{1}{2}'' \times 2\frac{3}{4}''$ (9 × 7 cm), the photographer would have paid about 9s. 6d. a dozen from his wholesale suppliers. These low prices applied only to the ambrotypes. Large portrait photographs on paper from the fashionable studios were far more expensive.

An interesting variation on the ambrotype was the 'Relievo' ambrotype which was appropriate for portraiture. Invented in 1857 by Thomas C. Lawrence the method involved removing the background so the black backing applied only to the area of the figure. By backing the plate with a separate piece of glass and white card, an effect of solidity could be given to the portrait.

For the decorative presentation of ambrotypes *Union Cases* were imported into England, following their patent by the American Samuel Peck, in 1854. Union cases were made from moulded plastic using a mixture of shellac, sawdust and pigment which, when heated, could be poured into a steel mould. On cooling the plastic mass set hard. The mould allowed for designs of fine detail, in relief, ranging from the geometric and pictorial to portraiture.

The spirit of the new manufacturing age when confident Victorians luxuriated in world supremacy was epitomized by one particular event; The Great Exhibition of the Industry of All Nations, staged in the magnificent purpose-built Crystal Palace at Hyde Park in London, in May 1851. The progress of the art and techniques of photography, a medium now just twelve years old, was given public attention and was used to record the event itself.

While visiting the Great Exhibition Queen Victoria admired a stereoscope and some stereoscopic photographs and following the example set by Her Majesty the public greeted this new invention with enthusiasm and thus began a craze that swept the world.

It is not difficult to understand the reasons for the popularity of stereoscopic photography. Literacy was increasing, and social conditions were improving. Railways were making travel easier, and more people had the means to take holidays away from the areas in which they lived and see other parts of their own country for the first time. For many, photography itself was a novelty, and the added attraction of being able to see the picture in three dimensions, was irresistible. It should be remembered that stereographs do not give an accurate picture of Victorian life. The beauty of the English countryside was frequently illustrated, but the poverty and derelict cottages were seldom shown. Views of Regency terraces in cities were more likely to sell than pictures of the squalor that existed in many of the industrial centres. The stereograph is as reliable as historical evidence as the picture postcard of today would be to a historian of the future.

Ambrotypes evolved into the *tintype* or *ferreotype* introduced by Adolphe Alexander Martin 1853 and made on a base of tinned or enamelled iron. It was a process much used by itinerant photographers, but few, if any, of the better establishments employed the method. Despite the poor quality of many of the results using this system, tintypes enjoyed a long run of popularity and were still being taken until recently by such operators as beach photographers.

Studio Portraits of Family Faces

Portrait of a dog posed for the camera.

Portrait of woman and baby.

Portrait of dolls with the inscription 'Jany (January) 30, 1858, focussed by Ruthey Ruff $5\frac{1}{4}$ years'. Miss Ruff was the daughter of the Brighton photographer George Ruff.

Portrait of young girls.

Portrait of young Welsh girls.

Portrait of young girl.

Portrait of Mary Vaughan Harke (1833–1909).

Portrait of young woman with stereoscope and stereo
cards as decorative objects.

Portrait of woman c. 1860.

Portrait of Miss E. S. Roper c. 1855.

Portrait of young girl by Brown, Baines and
Bell, Photographers to her Majesty at Liver-
pool, 1 July 1886.

Portrait of man with stereoscope as decorative object.

Portrait of Sir Herbert Benjamin Edwardes (1819–1868) with his wife by Ross and Thomson, Edinburgh c. 1860.

Portrait of man holding accordion as studio prop. An example of a 'Relievo' ambrotype.

Portrait of man and wife by Moule's Photographic Rooms, 15 Seabright Place, Hackney Road, (city unknown).

Portrait of members of the Young family.

Portrait of a young boy holding a cricket bat, standing in front of elaborate painted backdrop.

Portrait of young girl holding doll, standing in front of elaborate painted backdrop, by T. Snaith, Photographic artist of London Road, Leicester.

Portrait of young girl with dog.

Exceptionally

Rare Interiors

Robert Crawshay taken in 1860's.

Robert Crawshay, an amateur ambrotypist, and his brother in a Turkish bath taken in 1860's.

Interior view of a church. An example of a stereoscopic ambrotype.

Snapshots at Last!

Family in a row-boat.

Portrait of the itinerant photographers Low and Lonly showing their camera on a tripod and their mobile darkroom located on a beach.

Portrait of a group in horse-drawn vehicle, presumed to have been taken at Ascot.

Portrait of a group in horse-drawn vehicle, with horse in harness.

Portrait of young girls.

Portrait of children and animals in goat cart with goat in harness.

Portrait of Joseph Grange, a sawyer who died in 1907 aged 87 years c. 1880.

Portrait of family group (from the left) Hon. Julia Henrietta
Dutton, Hon. Emily Isabella Constance Dutton, Hon. and
Rev. Fred Dutton (later 5th Lord of Sherborne), Hon. Mary
Louise Dutton.

Portrait of Welsh family group.

Portrait of family group taken on 2 May 1863.

View of farmyard with men and fowl in foreground.

Portrait of men, children and dogs.

Portrait of Welsh men displaying working tools.

Portrait of men on a railway station inscribed 'Taken Sunday morning waiting for the pub to open. August 1877'.

View of shopfront of Wormull, a cutler of 121 Stanford Street, City of London. Elderly man with dogs presumed to be Wormull.

Portrait of school boys.

The Main Steps to Making an Ambrotype

The main steps to make a collodion negative in preparation for the Ambrotype called for great skill and care in the manipulation:

1 Polishing.
2 Covering with a thin coat of collodion and potassium iodide, and draining off the excess.
3 Sensitizing (in the darkroom) in a bath of silver-nitrate until it turned yellow.
4 Mounting (while still wet) in a dark slide.
5 Exposing in the camera by uncapping the lens for a measured time.
6 Removing from the dark slide (in the darkroom) and developing in pyrogallic acid.
7 Rinsing the developed negative in clean water.
8 Fixing in 'hypo' (hyposulphite of soda).
9 Washing thoroughly in running water.
10 Drying.
11 Finally (and optionally) varnishing to protect the emulsion.

The main steps to make the positive Ambrotype from the collodion negative:

1 Bleaching the negative in nitric acid or bichloride of mercury.
2 Washing thoroughly in running water.
3 Drying.
4 Backing the negative with black velvet, black paper or opaque varnish.
5 Drying the varnish.
6 Hand tinting the negative (optional).
7 Finally, assembling in frame or case.

BOOKS FOR FURTHER INFORMATION

The Story of Popular Photography by Colin Ford, Century Hutchinson, 1989

The Rise of Photography 1850–1880: The Age of Collodion by Helmut Gernsheim, Thames and Hudson, 1988

Crown and Camera: The Royal Family 1842–1910 by Francis Dimond and Roger Taylor, Penguin Books, 1987

The Ambrotype: Research into its Restoration and Conservation by Ian Moor, The Paper Conservator Volume 1, 1976

The Collodion Process on Glass by F. S. Archer. Enlarged, second edition published by Archer 1854.

Manual of the Collodion Photographic Process by F. S. Archer. Published by Archer 1851.

Cleaning and Repairing an Ambrotype

Ambrotypes are very easily restored. An ambrotype is nothing more than a glass negative held in front of a black backing by a brass frame. The backing might be of cloth, paper or paint; it is usually this which needs restoration.

1. Use cotton gloves and a clean surface for handling the ambrotype during repairing and cleaning. With an X-acto knife, pry the brass frame, with the image, out of its case. Pry carefully from all sides. When it is free, gently bend the frame and remove the ambrotype, cover glass and backing. Sometimes paper tape holds the ambrotype together. The glue is usually so dry the tape will fall off; but in stubborn cases, slit the tape with the knife to separate the contents.

2. Having removed the brass frame the four pieces of the ambrotype are revealed separately:
   the thick glass cover
   the thin brass matt
   the ambrotype negative on glass
   the thin black backing

3 If the backing is painted on the glass negative and appears cracked or crazed, it will have to be scraped off with a razor blade. Before you begin to scrape, make doubly sure that it is the backing you are scraping and not the negative emulsion. Black paper and cloth backing can be removed from the negative easily.

4. After the backing has been removed, clean both sides of the cover glass and the surface of the negative that does not have the emulsion (the negative image) on it. Use a soft cloth *dampened* with soapy distilled water. Make sure not to get any moisture on the emulsion side.

5. A new backing can be made from black paper, black velvet, or black plastic. Photographic paper comes in a black plastic bag that is a good, rich black, suitable for backing ambrotypes. Once the surfaces are cleaned and the new backing is made, reassemble the pieces and wrap the brass frame around them. Make sure the frame is tight. If it is too loosely wrapped, you may split the case when the frame and its contents are replaced. If the frame or case for the ambrotype is leather a good hide food should be applied to clean and polish the surface.

6. Copy photographs of ambrotypes are useful and you should make a copy of the ambrotype both before and after restoration.

A c k n o w l e d g m e n t s

Photographs are reproduced by courtesy of the Royal Photographic Society, Bath
pages 12, 15, 22, 24, 25, 26, 39, 41, 45

By courtesy of the Museum of London
pages 13, 38, 44

By courtesy of the National Portrait Gallery, London
pages 14, 16, 21, 34, 35

By courtesy of the Welsh Folk Museum, Cardiff
pages 15, 40, 42

By courtesy of the Board of Trustees of the Victoria and Albert Museum, London
pages 18, 19, 23, 28, 29

By permission of the Trustees of the Science Museum, London
pages 6, 7, 8, 9, 10, 32

By courtesy of a private collector
pages 14, 17, 20, 21, 30, 33, 36, 37, 40, 43

Captions to the text illustrations p.7, 8, 9, 10

An early photograph on glass taken by Sir John Herschel in September 1839.

The photograph, copied from a publication, shows scaffolding around a telescope.

A Thomas box tent for ambrotype photography.

Portable dark tent for ambrotype photography c. 1860.

A stereoscope made by Hirst and Wood, London 1862.